How Do You Investigate?

HOUGHTON MIFFLIN HARCOURT

PHOTOGRAPHY CREDITS: (r) ©Thomas Northcut/Photodisc/Getty Images; ©Andersen Ross/Blend Images/Corbis; 3 (c) ©Alamy Images Royalty Free; 4 (b) ©Comstock/Getty Images

Printed in Mexico

ISBN: 978-0-544-07218-3

12 0908 20 19 18 17

4500669231   A B C D E F G

Be an Active Reader!

 Look at these words.

senses	thermometer
investigation	inquiry skills
science tools	

 Look for answers to these questions.

What are the five senses?

How do you use your senses?

What happens when you observe?

What do scientists do?

What is a science tool?

How can you record what you learn?

How do you use inquiry skills?

What are the five senses?

Senses help you learn about the world around you. You have five senses. The senses are sight, hearing, smell, touch, and taste.

Which sense or senses is this child using?

How do you use your senses?

You use your senses all the time. You hear music with your ears. You taste food with your mouth. You see what is in front of you with your eyes. You smell things with your nose. You touch things with your hands and skin.

see

hear

smell

taste

touch

The child observes a dog playing.

What happens when you observe?

When you observe, you watch things. You see a nest. What bird made it? You can watch the nest. You may see the bird.

Does a dog like a toy? You can watch her. Does she chase the toy? You can observe lots of things in nature!

What do scientists do?

Scientists want to know about the world. They ask questions. They try to find answers. To learn more, they do an investigation. This means they plan a test. There are all kinds of scientists. All of them study and observe things.

Scientists study the needs of living things.

Does the sun warm the water?

Scientists ask questions. Some science questions have numbers as answers.

You can ask a science question. On a warm day, does the sun help warm up water? You can do an investigation. Your answer should have numbers.

What is a science tool?

Science tools help you learn. A measuring cup measures liquid. A thermometer tells how hot or cold something is.

Put one cup of water in two glasses. How hot or cold is the water in each glass? Put one glass of water in the sun and one in the shade.

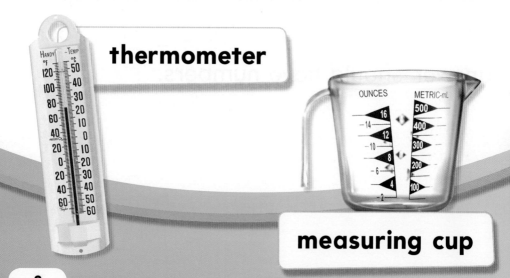

thermometer

measuring cup

How can you record what you learn?

You can use numbers, pictures, or words to record what you observe.

The chart below shows possible temperatures for each cup. Make a chart for the temperatures in your cups.

Time	Cup 1 (Sun)	Cup 2 (Shade)
11:00	33 °F	33 °F
11:30	37 °F	35 °F
12:00	43 °F	40 °F
12:30	50 °F	47 °F
1:00	65 °F	56 °F
1:30	72 °F	60 °F
2:00	75 °F	62 °F

What does the chart show?

Look at the chart. Look at the temperatures for each time. Did they go up or down? They went up every time. Did they go up the same for both cups? No. The temperature of the water in the shade did not go up as much.

You have an answer to the science question. The sun helped warm up the water.

Time	Cup 1 (Sun)	Cup 2 (Shade)
11:00	33 °F	33 °F
11:30	37 °F	35 °F
12:00	43 °F	40 °F
12:30	50 °F	47 °F
1:00	65 °F	56 °F
1:30	72 °F	60 °F
2:00	75 °F	62 °F

Inquiry Skills

observe ✔

ask a science question ✔

plan an investigation ✔

measure ✔

compare ✔

predict -- say what you think will happen ✔

How do you use inquiry skills?

You use inquiry skills to help you find out information. Inquiry skills help you learn what the sun does to water temperature. You can work like a scientist!

Stay Safe!

Some science tools are safer to use than others. Brainstorm ways to stay safe when doing an investigation. Make a list of safety rules.

Draw a Graph

Think about something in nature that you would like to observe. Ask your teacher to help you think of an idea. Draw your observations as a picture graph. For instance, observe how many dogs you see during a single day. Record when, where, and how many you saw.